PIANO/VOCAL SELECTIONS

THE Will Rogers FOLLIES
A Life in Revue

PIERRE COSSETTE
MARTIN RICHARDS   SAM CROTHE[...]
JAMES M. NEDERLANDER   STEWART F. LANE   MAX[...]
in association with JAPAN SATELLITE BROADCA[...]

present

KEITH CARRADINE

in

Book by **PETER STONE**

Music Composed & Arranged by **CY COLEMAN**

Lyrics by **BETTY COMDEN** and **ADOLPH GREEN**

Also Starring

DEE HOTY

with

DICK LATESSA   CADY HUFFMAN

VINCE BRUCE   THE WILL ROGERS WRANGLERS   THE MAD CAP MUTTS   PAUL UKENA, JR.

featuring

THE NEW ZIEGFELD GIRLS

with

the special participation of **GREGORY PECK** as the voice of Mr. Ziegfeld

Inspired by the words of **WILL** and **BETTY ROGERS**

Settings Design **TONY WALTON**   Costume Design **WILLA KIM**   Lighting Design **JULES FISHER**

Sound Design **PETER FITZGERALD**   Projection Design **WENDALL K. HARRINGTON**   Wig Design **HOWARD LEONARD**

Orchestrations **BILLY BYERS**   Musical Direction **ERIC STERN**   Musical Contractor **JOHN MILLER**

General Management **MARVIN A. KRAUSS ASSOCIATES, INC.**   General Press Representative **JUDY JACKSINA**

Casting by **JULIE HUGHES** and **BARRY MOSS, CSA**   Production Stage Manager **PETER VON MAYRHAUSER**

Associate Director **PHILLIP OESTERMAN**   Associate Choreographer **JEFF CALHOUN**

Directed and Choreographed by

TOMMY TUNE

Original Cast Album on Columbia Records

Cover Art © 1991 Serino Coyne, Inc. LOGO DESIGN BY DEWYNTERS, PLC

ISBN-13: 978-1-4234-2855-8
ISBN-10: 1-4234-2855-2

HAL•LEONARD® CORPORATION
7777 W. BLUEMOUND RD. P.O. BOX 13819 MILWAUKEE, WI 53213

For info on Notable Music Co. Inc./The Cy Coleman Office, visit www.cycoleman.com and www.myspace.com/cycoleman

Visit Hal Leonard Online at
www.halleonard.com

Cy Coleman

Cy Coleman was a musician's composer, classically trained at piano, composition, and orchestration at New York City's High School for the Performing Arts and NY College of Music. Mr. Coleman was being groomed to be the next great conductor. Instead he turned his passion to jazz and formed the popular Cy Coleman Trio. Born Seymour Kaufman on June 14, 1929 in the Bronx, he changed his name at age 16 in time to use it on his first compositions with lyricist Joe A. McCarthy ("Why Try to Change Me Now," and "I'm Gonna Laugh You Right out of My Life"). While still performing in jazz clubs and enjoying a successful recording career, Cy began writing with veteran songwriter Carolyn Leigh. Hits like "Witchcraft" and "The Best Is Yet to Come" were followed by their leap to Broadway with *Wildcat,* starring Lucille Ball ("Hey, Look Me Over") and then *Little Me* ("I've Got Your Number" and "Real Live Girl"). In 1966 Cy, along with legendary lyricist Dorothy Fields, triumphed with the smash hit *Sweet Charity* ("Big Spender," "If My Friends Could See Me Now"). Cy continued on Broadway and wrote the scores for *Seesaw, I Love My Wife, On the Twentieth Century, Barnum, City of Angels, The Will Rogers Follies,* and *The Life.* In 2004 Cy returned to his roots and revived the Cy Coleman Trio, once again wowing the audiences with his amazing skill at the piano. In Mr. Coleman's amazing career he took home three Tony® Awards, two GRAMMY Awards®, three Emmy® Awards, an Academy Award® nomination, and countless honors. Cy served on the Board of ASCAP for three decades.

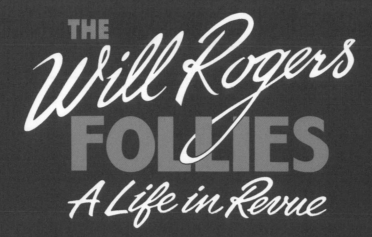

THE
Will Rogers
FOLLIES
A Life in Revue

CONTENTS

WILLAMANIA

Music by CY COLEMAN
Lyrics by BETTY COMDEN and ADOLPH GREEN

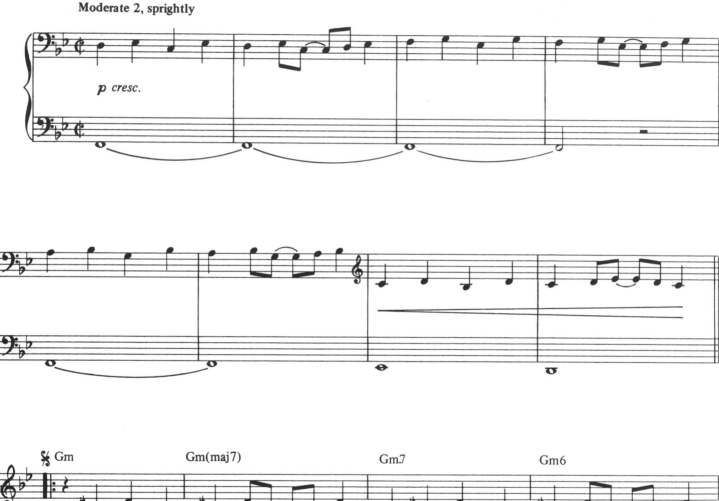

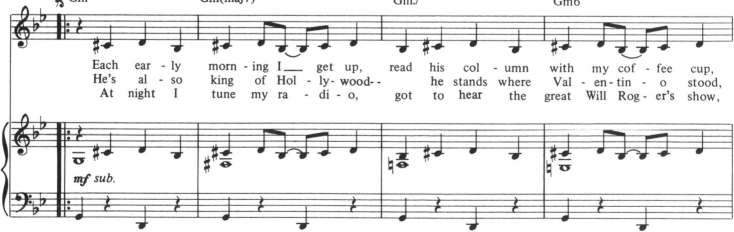

Each ear-ly morn-ing I__ get up, read his col-umn with my cof-fee cup,
He's al-so king of Hol-ly-wood-- he stands where Val-en-tin-o stood,
At night I tune my ra-di-o, got to hear the great Will Rog-er's show,

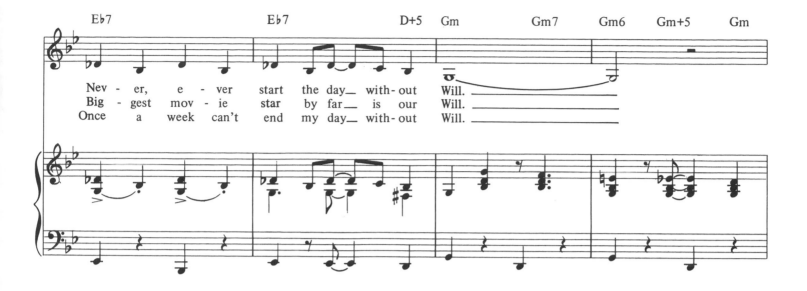

Nev - er, e - ver start the day_ with-out Will._____
Big - gest mov - ie star by far_ is our Will._____
Once a week can't end my day_ with-out Will._____

His wit and wis - dom let__ me see all the foi - bles of this cen - tur - y.
At an - y - time a - round_ the clock lines keep form-ing all a - round_ the block.
Rush home so I won't get __ there late 'cause I've got a ver - y spec - ial date,

There's no way to start my day_ with-out Will._____
Watch them fill the mov - ie till__ for our Will._____
Once a week the night be-longs_ to my Will._____

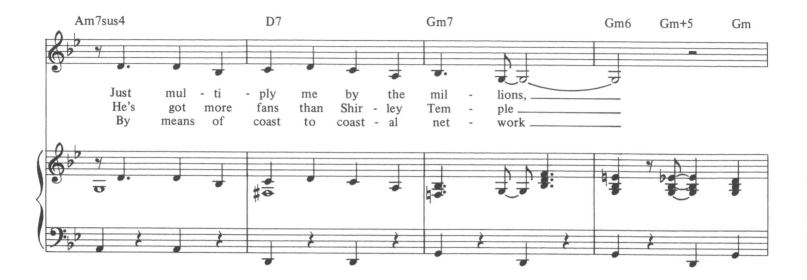

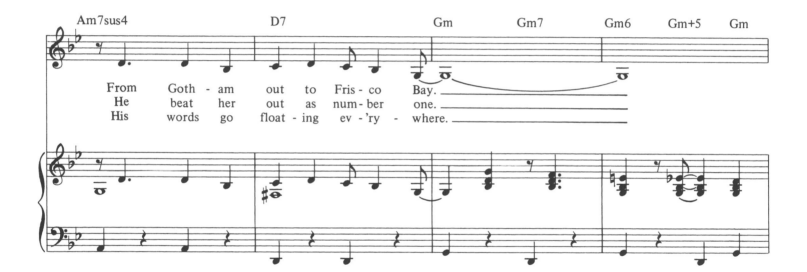

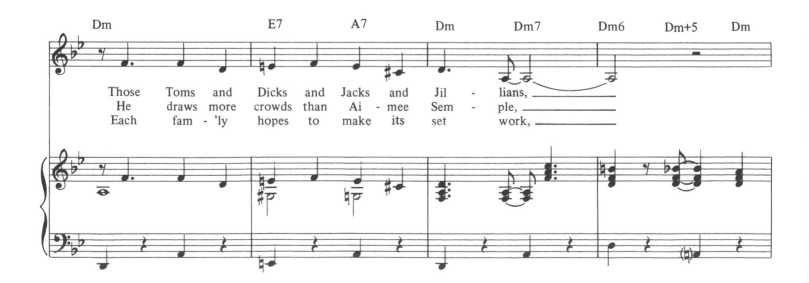

Are ask-ing, "Hey, did you see what Will said to-day?"__
the coun-try'd ra-ther do the dance that Wills' be-gun.__
so they can say, "D'ja hear what Will said on the air?"__

To Coda

Will-a-man-ia!__ This dance has swept the na-tion,

Will-a-man-ia!__ Dance of com-mu-ni-ca-tion.

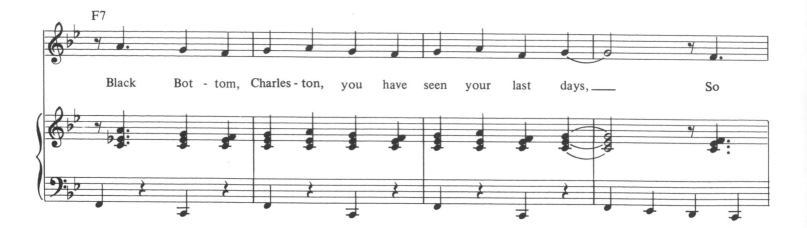

Black Bot - tom, Charles - ton, you have seen your last days, ___ So

scratch your skull, tilt your head, and do the new craze. We call it;

Will - a - man - ia! ___ It's in - ter - con - tin - en - tal,

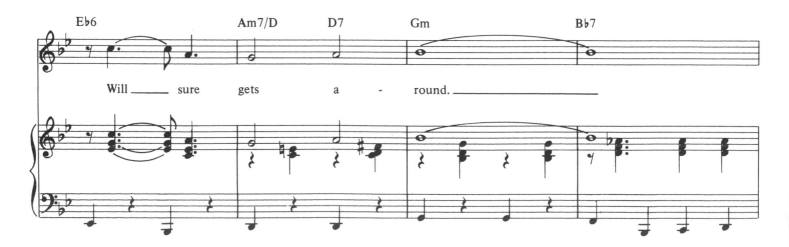

Will ___ sure gets a - round. _____

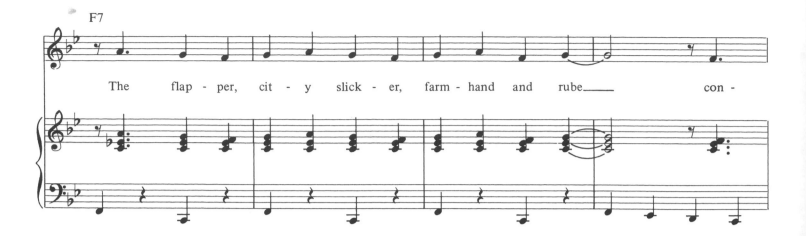

The flap - per, cit - y slick - er, farm - hand and rube____ con -

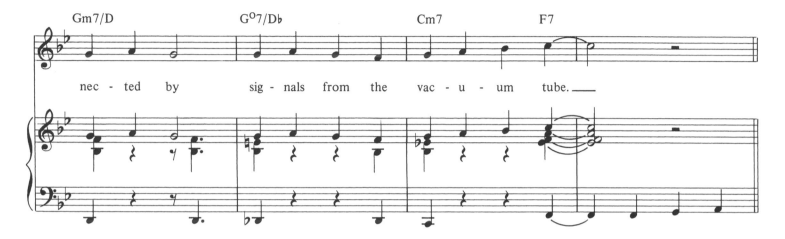

nec - ted by sig - nals from the vac - u - um tube.____

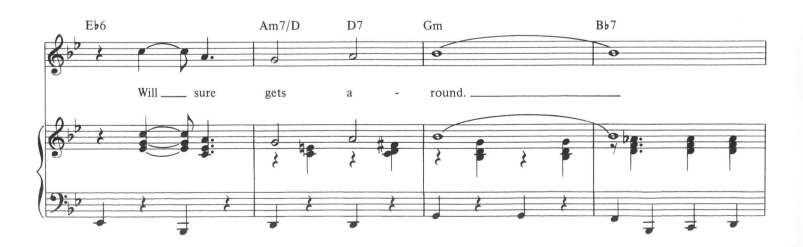

Will - a - man - ia!____ He's al - so hit the White House,

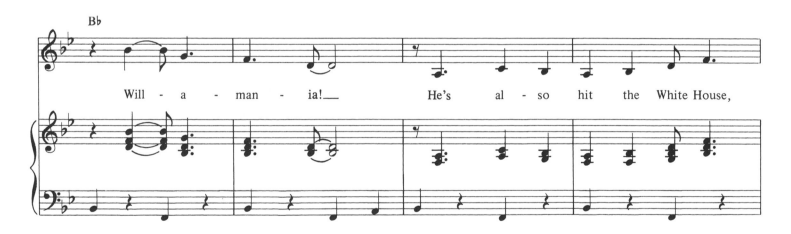

Will ____ sure gets a - round. _____

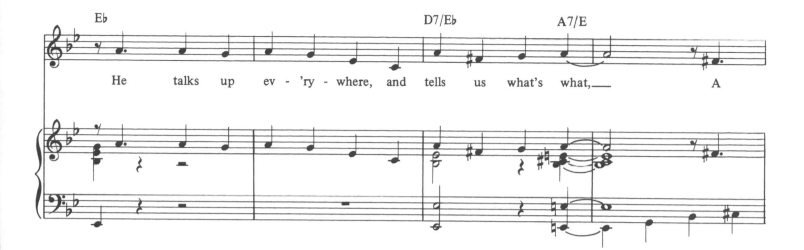

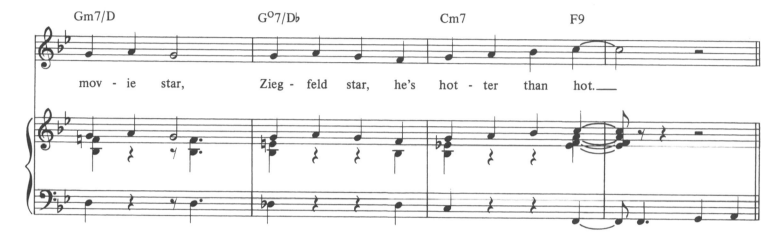

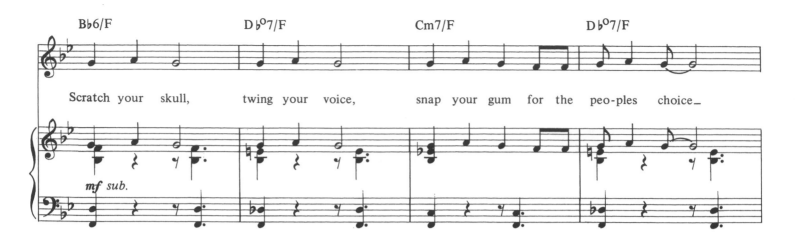

Scratch your skull, twing your voice, snap your gum for the peo-ples choice

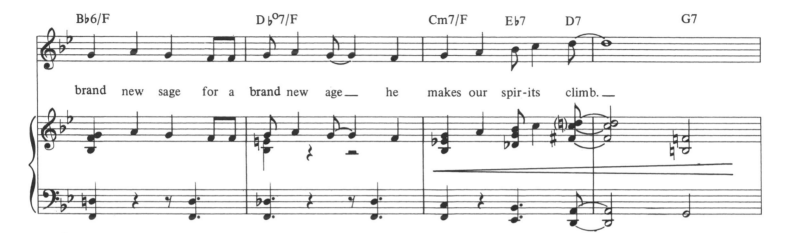

brand new sage for a brand new age he makes our spir-its climb.

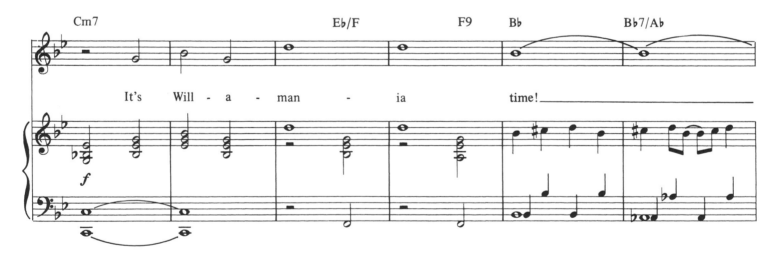

It's Will-a-man-ia time!

GIVE A MAN ENOUGH ROPE

Music by CY COLEMAN
Lyrics by BETTY COMDEN and ADOLPH GREEN

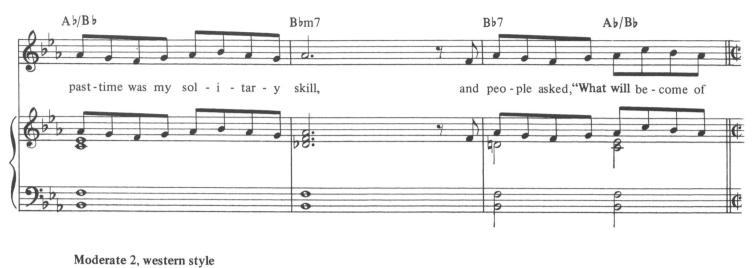

past-time was my sol - i - tar - y skill, and peo - ple asked, "What will be - come of

Moderate 2, western style

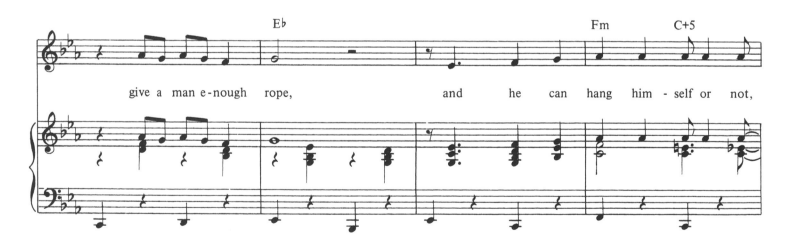

Will?" Give a man e - nough rope,

give a man e - nough rope, and he can hang him - self or not,

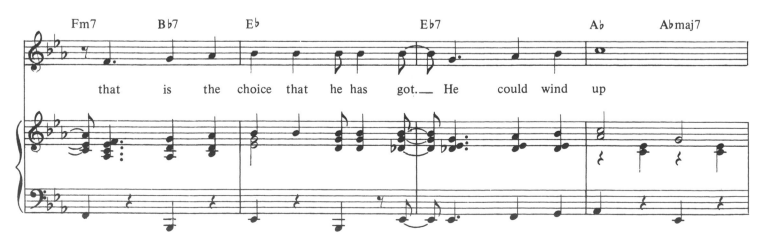

that is the choice that he has got.__ He could wind up

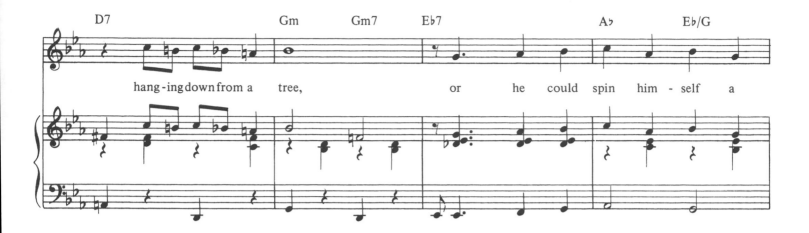

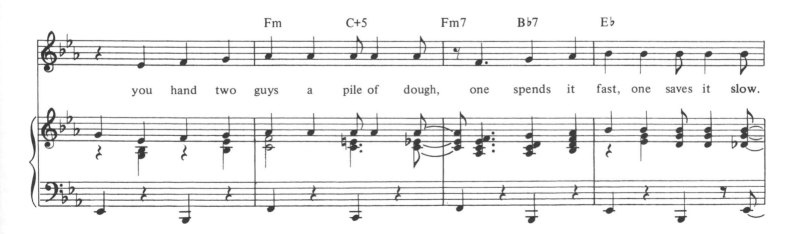

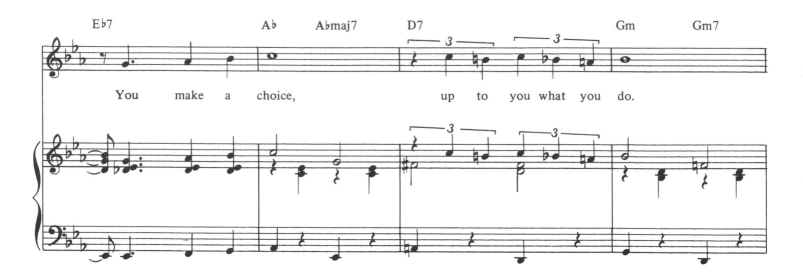

You make a choice, up to you what you do.

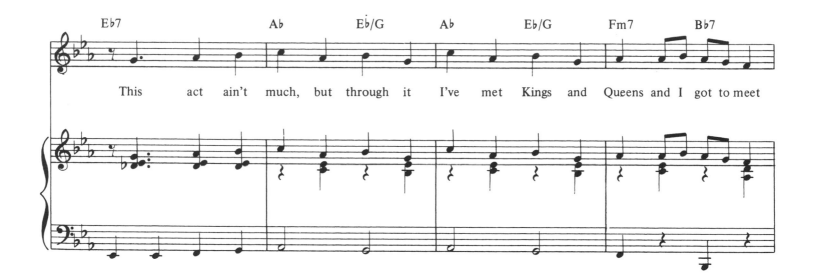

This act ain't much, but through it I've met Kings and Queens and I got to meet

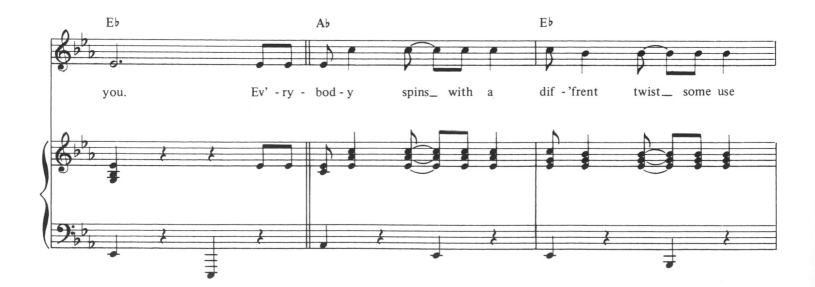

you. Ev' - ry - bod - y spins_ with a dif -'frent twist_ some use

el - bow grease,_ some just flick the wrist._ If you want to aim_ for a

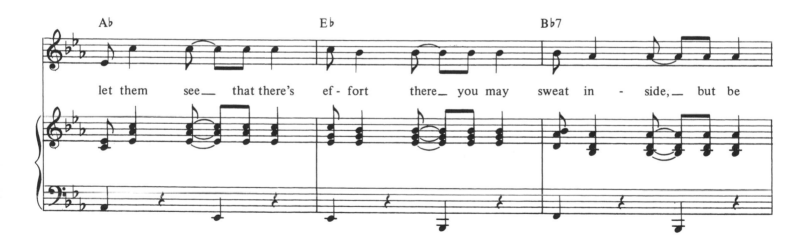

great big "O"._ go for broke, just let 'er go.__ Nev - er

let them see_ that there's ef - fort there_ you may sweat in - side,_ but be

de - bon - air__ If you go for tears_ or you go for jokes,_ shrug it

off, "It's noth - in' folks."_ Give a man e - nough rope,

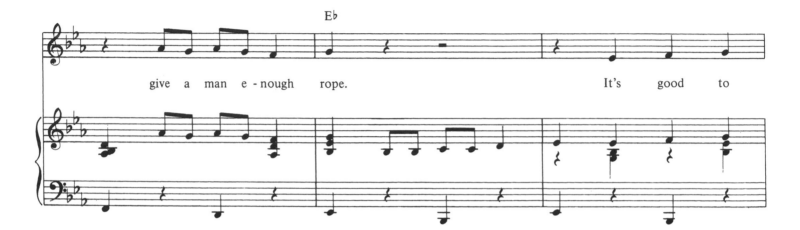

give a man e - nough rope. It's good to

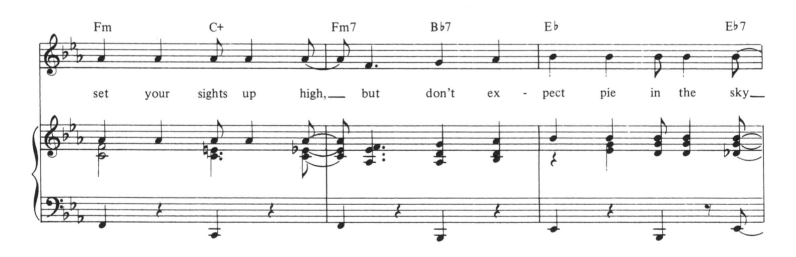

set your sights up high,_ but don't ex - pect pie in the sky_

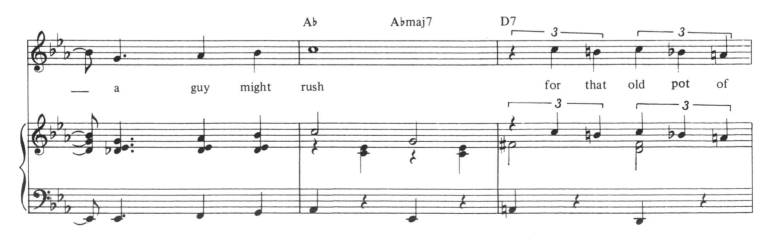

_ a guy might rush for that old pot of

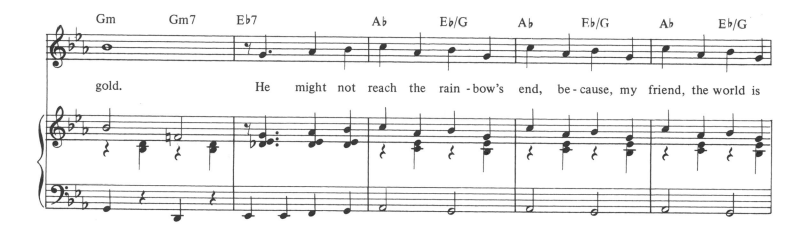

gold. He might not reach the rain-bow's end, be-cause, my friend, the world is

round, or so__ we are told._____ A guy could choose to run a

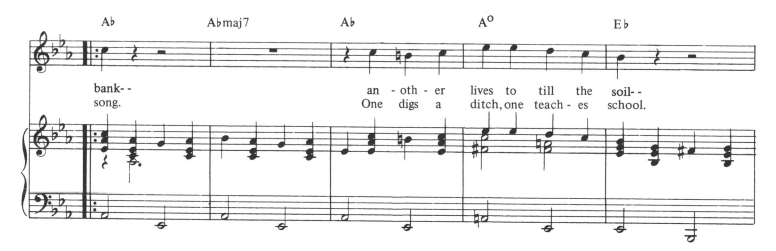

bank-- ....an -oth- er lives to till the soil--
song. One digs a ditch, one teach-es school.

or prac-tice law, or vi-o-lin--
But from the day I came a-

IT'S A BOY

Music by CY COLEMAN
Lyrics by BETTY COMDEN and ADOLPH GREEN

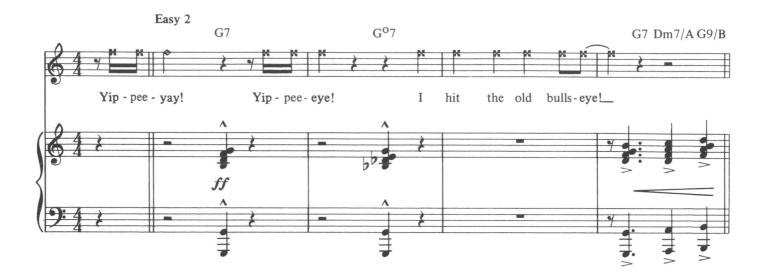

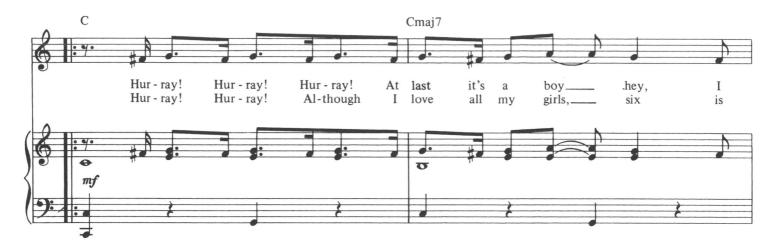

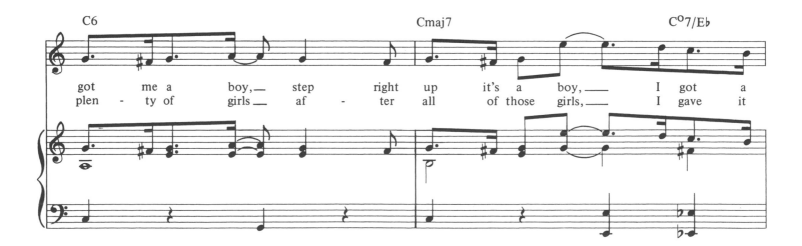

His pa's a ranch-er so he'll be the same.__ With cat-tle stand-ing out

yon-der for miles__ a-round, that's why I'm hand-ing the smokes and the smiles__ a-round.

Hur-ray! Hur-ray! Hur-ray at last it's a male__ and his pow-er-ful wail__ says he's

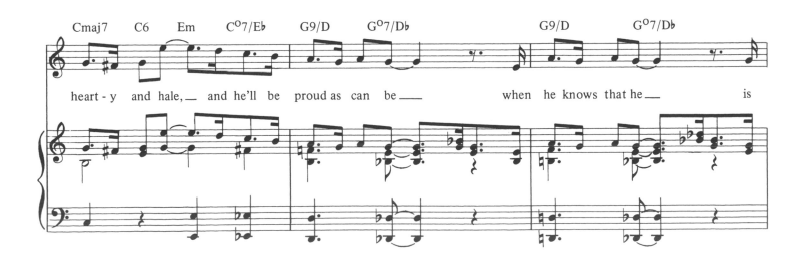

heart-y and hale,__ and he'll be proud as can be __ when he knows that he__ is

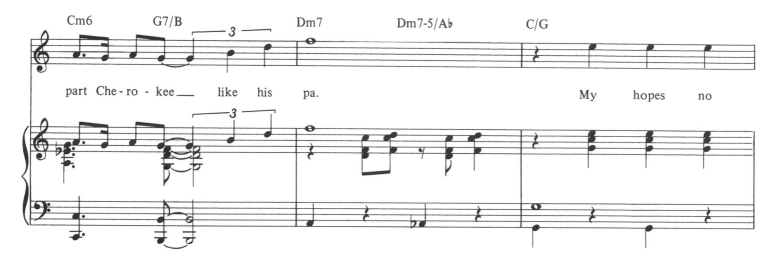

part Che - ro - kee___ like his pa. My hopes no

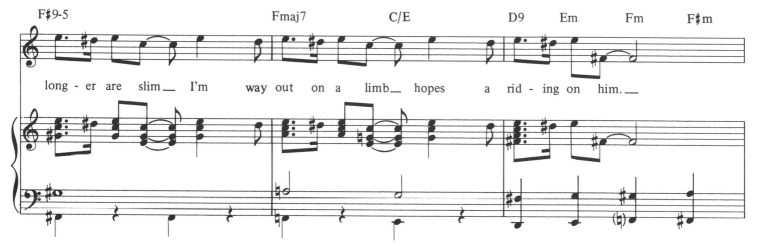

long - er are slim___ I'm way out on a limb___ hopes a rid - ing on him.___

And he'll grow up in - to a hell - uv - a man,___ I'll make him a man,___ a

hell - uv - a man___ like yours tru - ly. Hur - ray! Hur - ray! Hur - ray! For

cresc. poco a poco

my luck-y star,___ have a ci - gar,___ I'm jump-ing for joy___

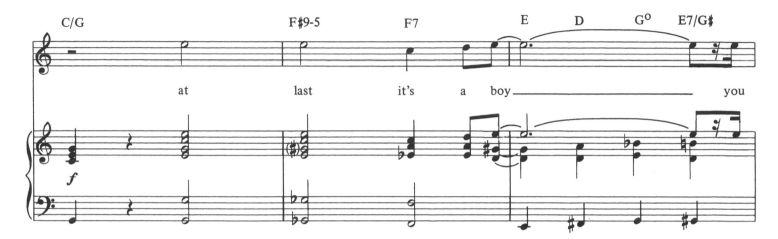

at last it's a boy_____ you

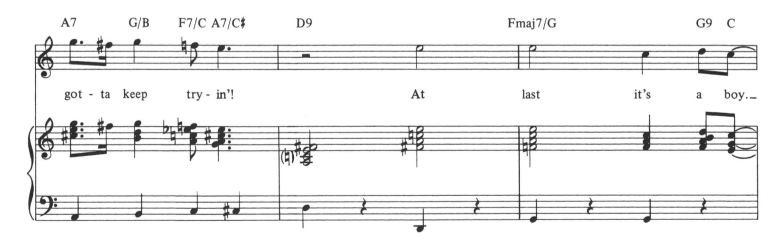

got - ta keep try - in'! At last it's a boy.__

MY UNKNOWN SOMEONE

Music by CY COLEMAN
Lyrics by BETTY COMDEN and ADOLPH GREEN

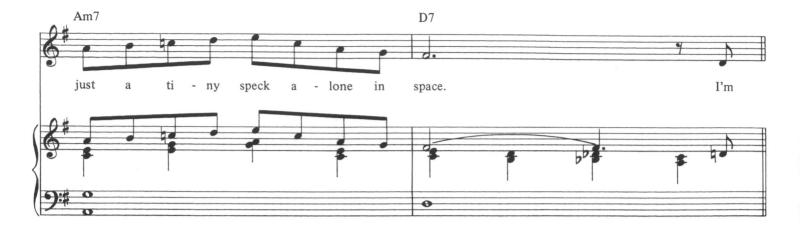

just a ti - ny speck a - lone in space. I'm

Moderate Ballad with feeling

drift - ing, I'm float - ing, a leaf in the wind- - an aim - less seed - ling sail - ing on the

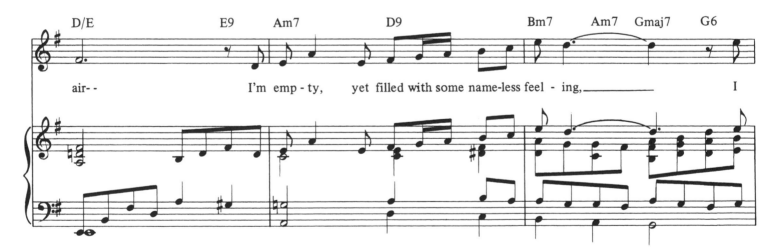

air- - I'm emp - ty, yet filled with some name-less feel - ing, _____ I

ache to come to rest some - where. In some - one's arms, _____ in

some-one's heart, some un-known some-one's life some-where- - My

ho-urs are end-less, my days have no shape,___ my nights are spent at moon-lit sol-i-

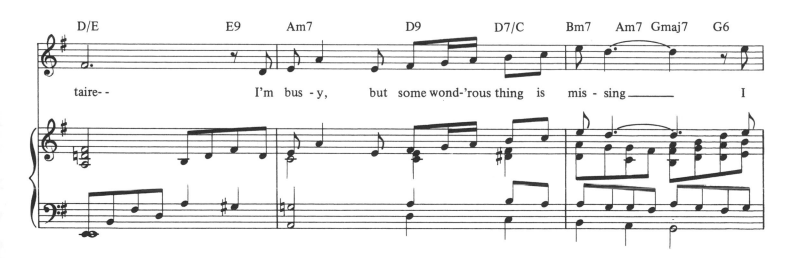

taire- - I'm bus-y, but some wond-'rous thing is mis-sing_____ I

long for,- - I don't know,_ but I know it must be there, in some-one's eyes, in

some-one's smile,___ a face I'll see some-day, some-where-- I'm

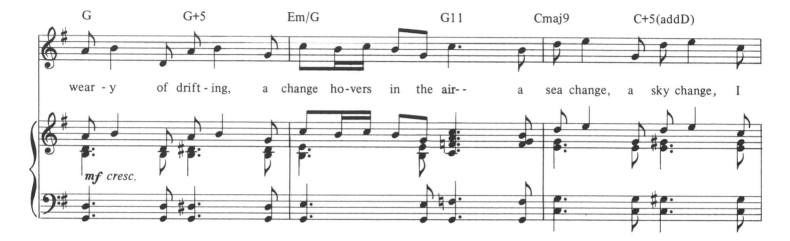

wear-y of drift-ing, a change ho-vers in the air-- a sea change, a sky change, I

feel that it's al-most there-- My jour-ney's end, lov-er, friend, my

un-known some-one some-where._____

THE BIG TIME

Music by CY COLEMAN
Lyrics by BETTY COMDEN and ADOLPH GREEN

What's to fear— we're to-geth-er here— but my dear be-fore— we can go

vau - de-ville— has tra - di - tions my young wife— ought to know. There's the

Start slow and accel.

small time— and the me - di - um time — and the

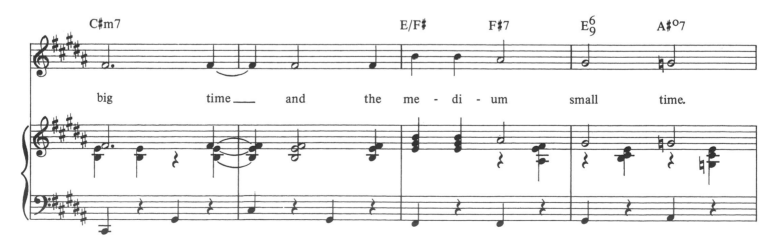

big time — and the me - di - um small time.

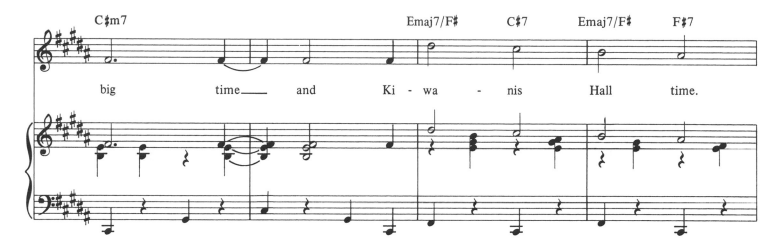

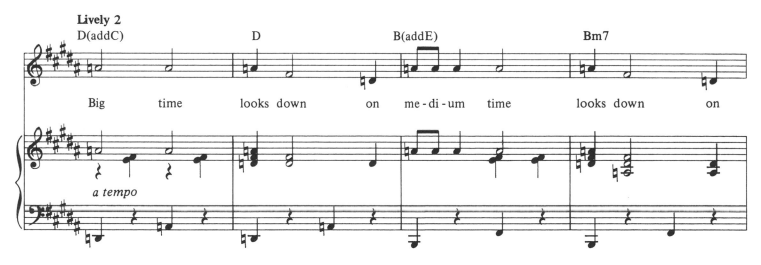

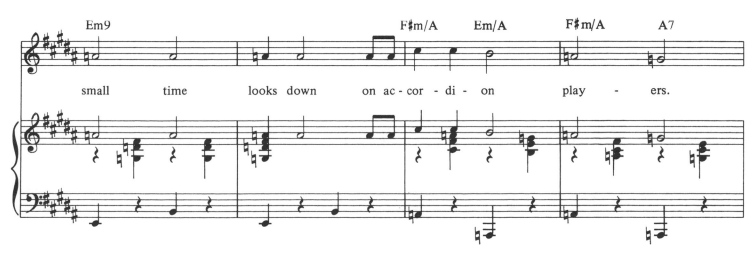

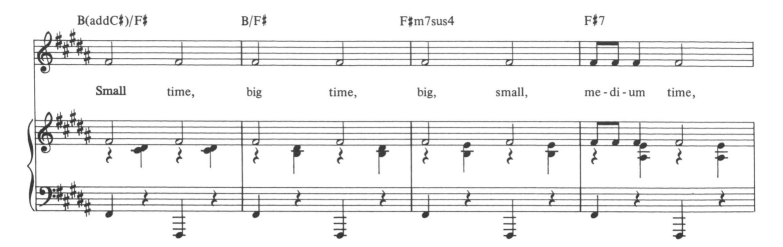

Small time, big time, big, small, me-di-um time,

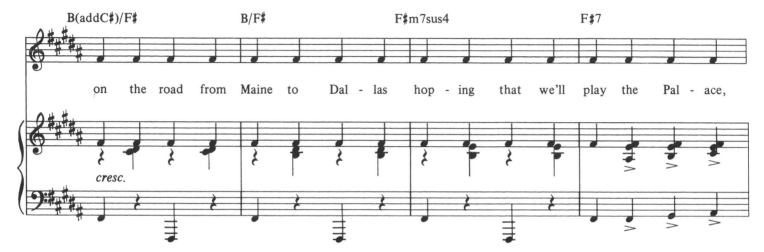

on the road from Maine to Dal-las hop-ing that we'll play the Pal-ace,

Smiles from you___ are a rave re-view___ put a

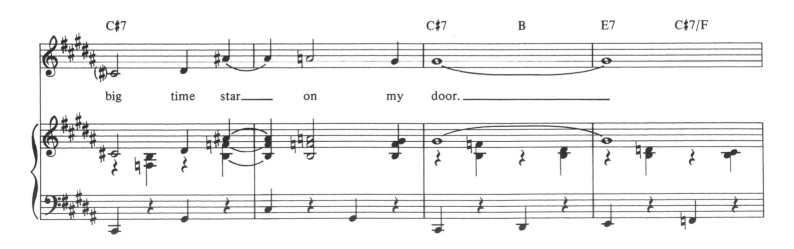

big time star___ on my door.___

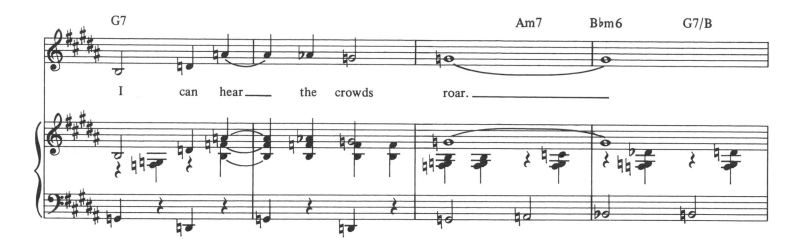

I can hear ___ the crowds roar. ___

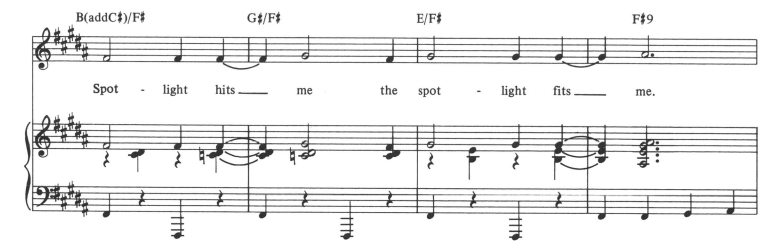

Spot - light hits ___ me the spot - light fits ___ me.

When you touch ___ me and when you hold ___ me my

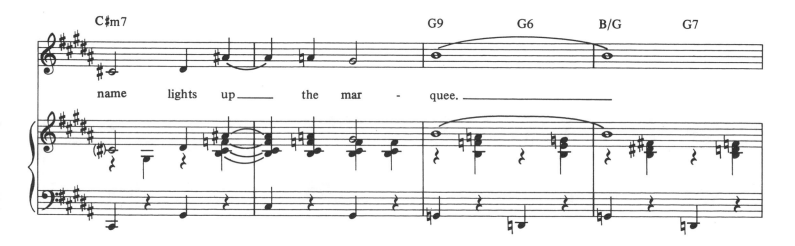

name lights up ___ the mar - quee. ___

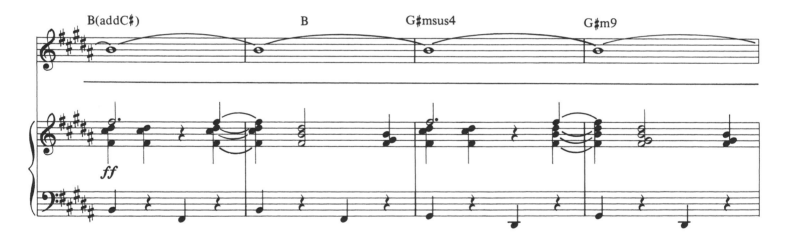

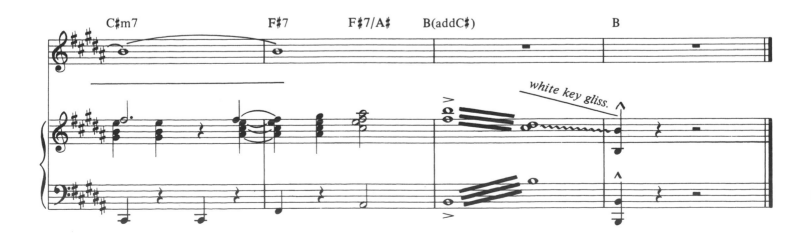

MY BIG MISTAKE

Music by CY COLEMAN
Lyrics by BETTY COMDEN and ADOLPH GREEN

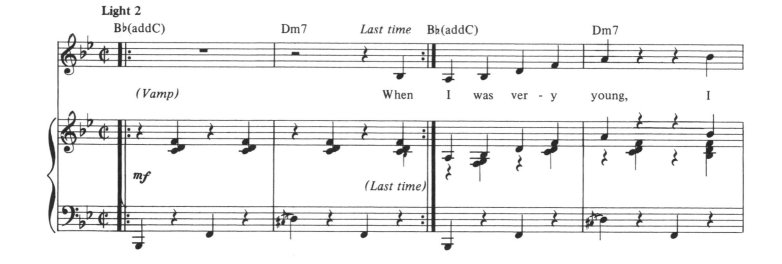

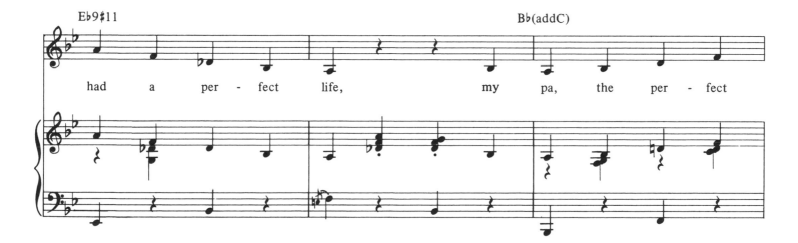

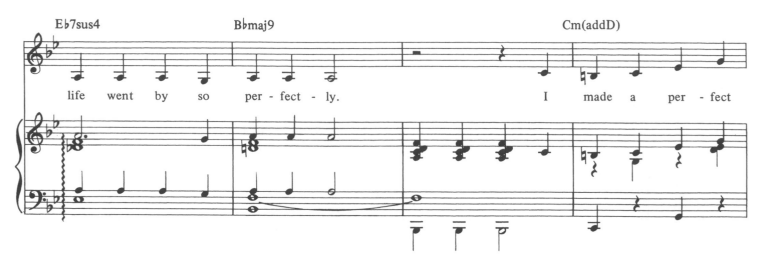

life went by so per - fect - ly. I made a per - fect

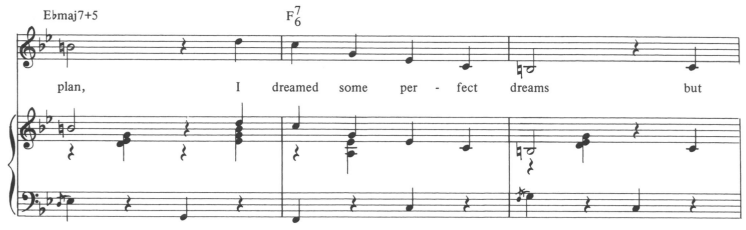

plan, I dreamed some per - fect dreams but

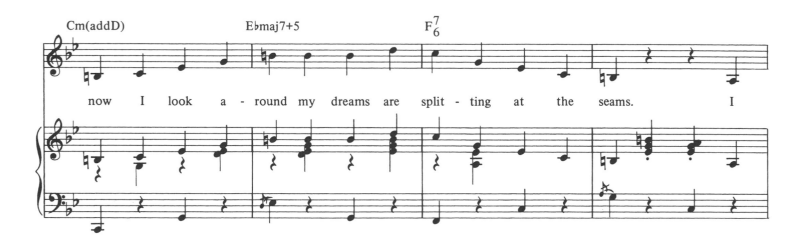

now I look a - round my dreams are split - ting at the seams. I

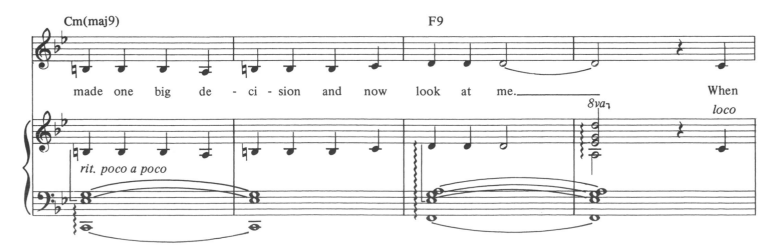

made one big de - ci - sion and now look at me. When

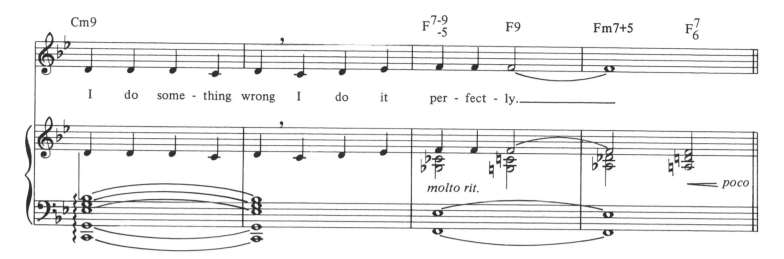

I do some-thing wrong I do it per-fect-ly._____

molto rit.

Relaxed Ballad in 2 (♩ = 60)

My big mis-take_____ rop-in' you in,_____

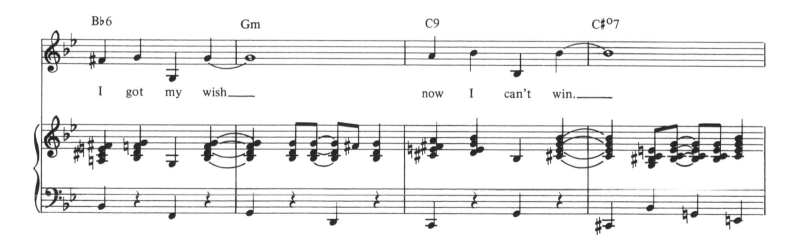

I got my wish_____ now I can't win._____

I thought once I caught_ you you'd quit your roam - in'_____

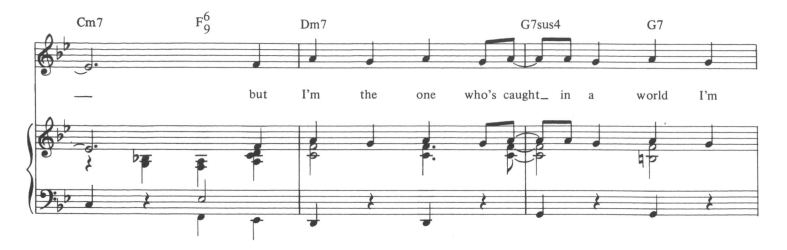

but I'm the one who's caught_ in a world I'm

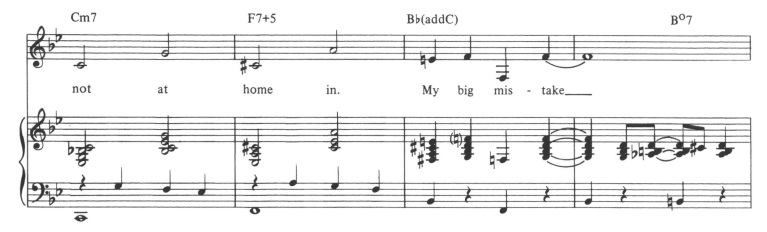

not at home in. My big mis - take____

think - in' you'd change,____ fan - cy - in' life____

— home on the range.____ 'Cause I like days all care-

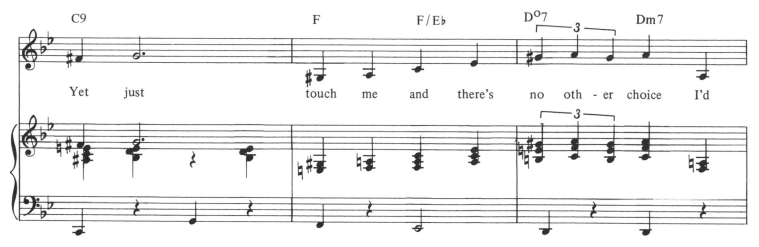

MARRY ME NOW

Music by CY COLEMAN
Lyrics by BETTY COMDEN and ADOLPH GREEN

Mar - ry me now,___ mar - ry me then,___

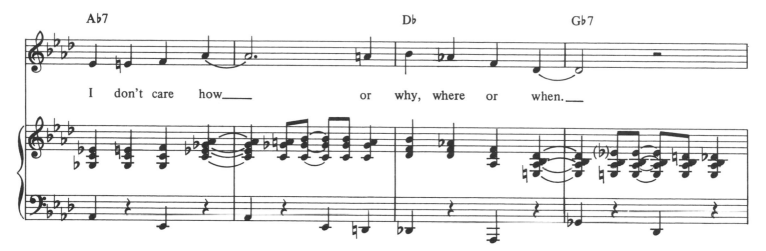

I don't care how___ or why, where or when.___

An - y - time you ask___ me I'll rush to the al - tar___ won't e - ven

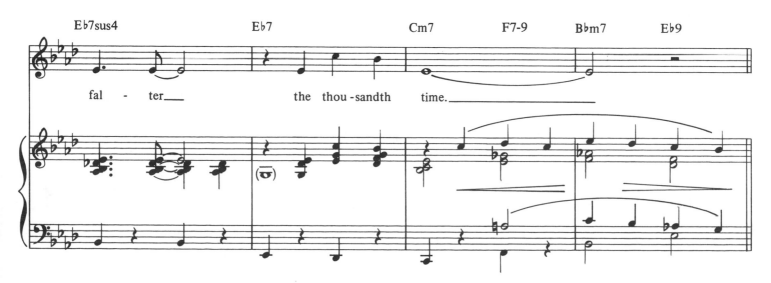

fal - ter___ the thou - sandth time.___

44

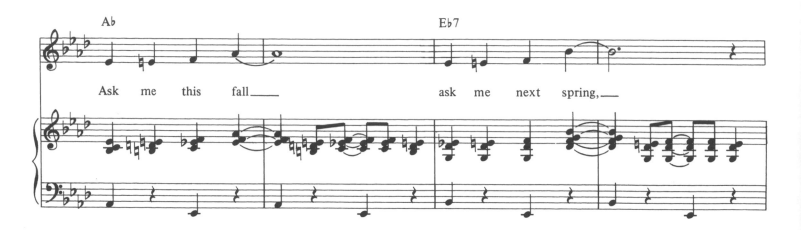

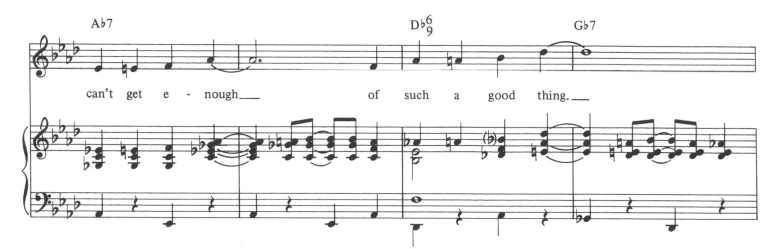

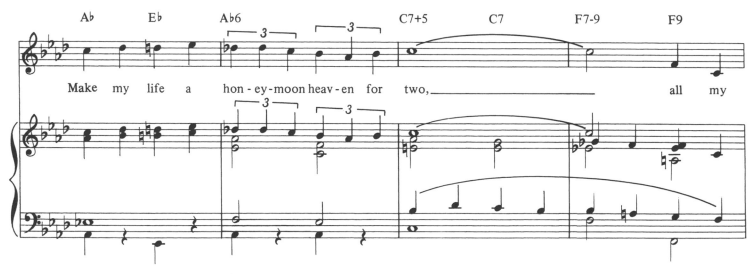

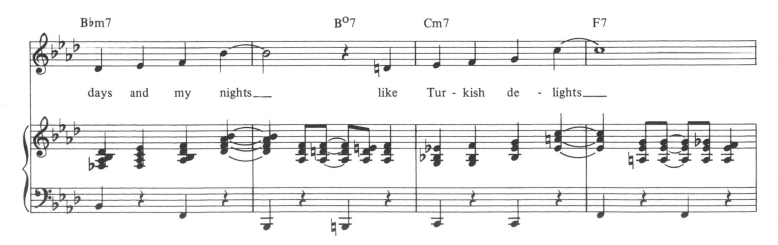

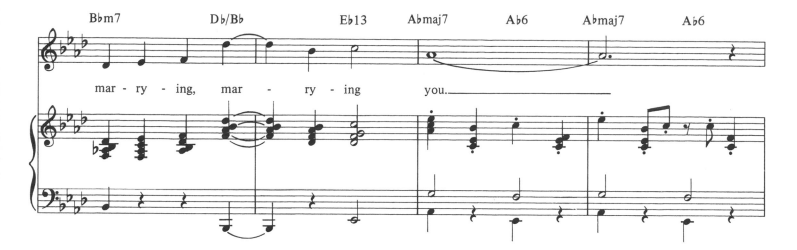

marry - ing, mar - ry - ing you._____

BETTY:

I got you... for the sec - ond time,

with a swing feel

I got you... it's our sec - ond splice, I got you...

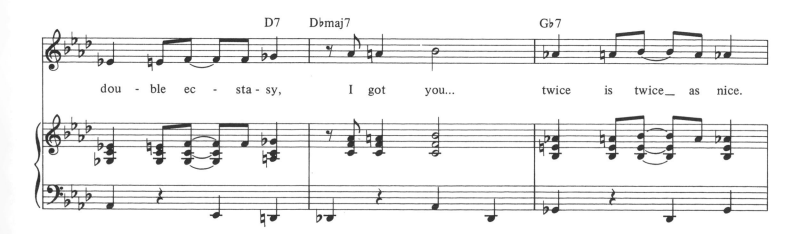

dou - ble ec - sta - sy, I got you... twice is twice__ as nice.

Down to the al - tar I'll si - dle,

I feel twice as brid - al. No shy vi - 'let, let's___ mid - dle aisle it.

I got you... and I'm twice_ as glad, I got you... like I did___ be - fore,

I got you... once is not___ e - nough, I got you...

so I'm back_ for more. We'll   have

a hon-ey-moon heav-en,   till a hun-dred and sev-en.

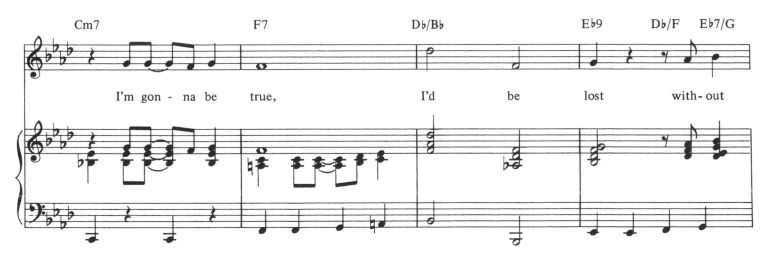

I'm gon-na be   true,   I'd   be   lost   with-out

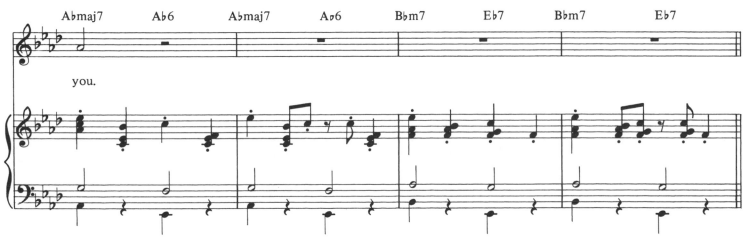

you.

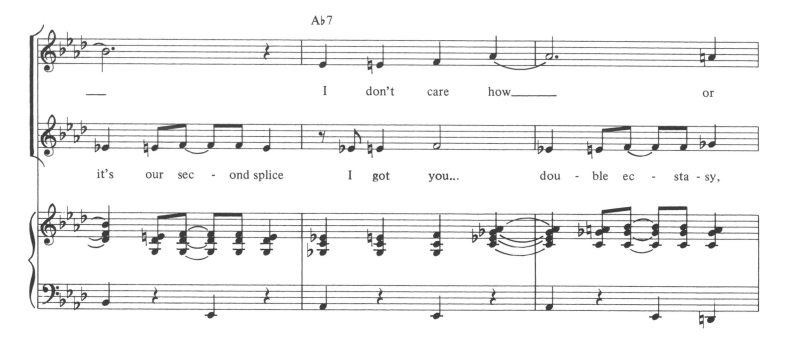

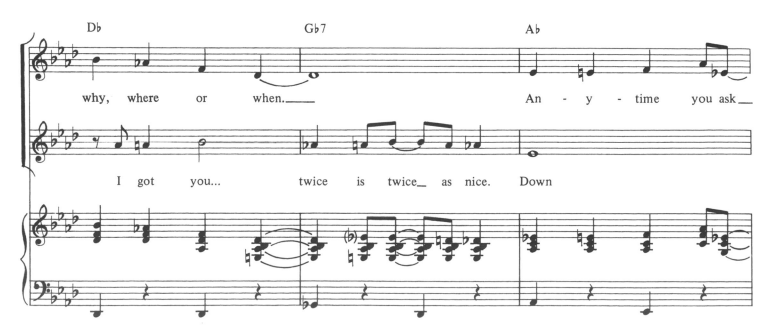

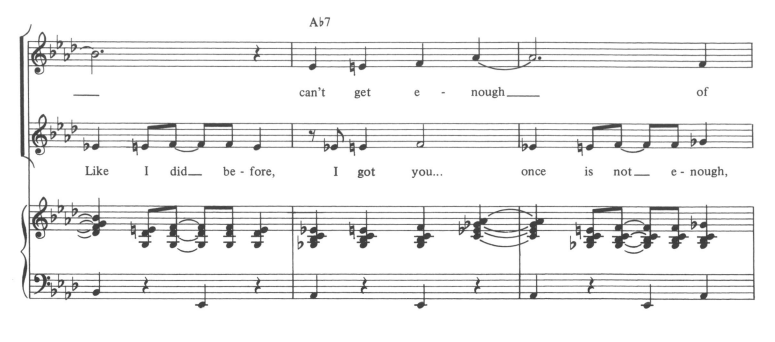

can't get e - nough____ of

Like I did__ be - fore, I got you... once is not__ e - nough,

such a good thing.__ Make my life a hon - ey - moon heav - en for

I got you... so I'm back_ for more. We'll have

two,_____ all my days and my nights__

a hon - ey - moon heav - en_____ till a hun - dred and

LOOK AROUND

Music by CY COLEMAN
Lyrics by BETTY COMDEN and ADOLPH GREEN

OUR FAVORITE SON

Music by CY COLEMAN
Lyrics by BETTY COMDEN and ADOLPH GREEN

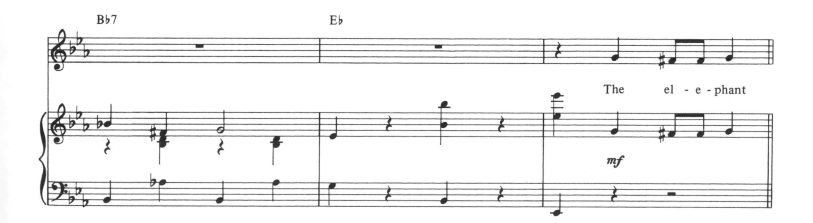

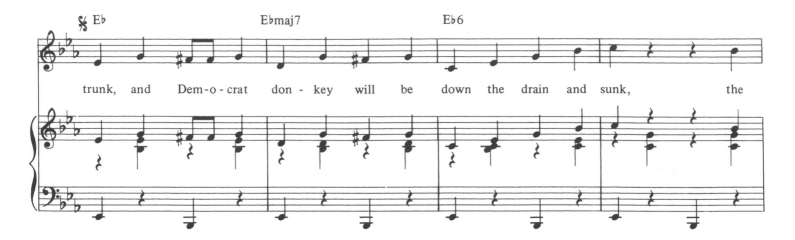

trunk, and Dem-o-crat don-key will be down the drain and sunk, the

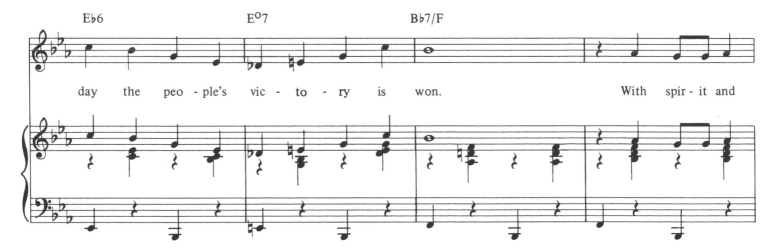

day the peo-ple's vic-to-ry is won. With spir-it and

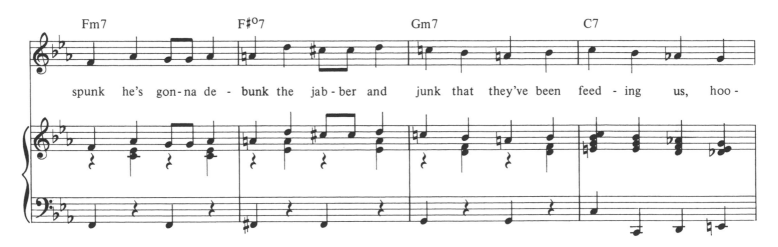

spunk he's gon-na de-bunk the jab-ber and junk that they've been feed-ing us, hoo-

ray for our fav-or-ite son! You

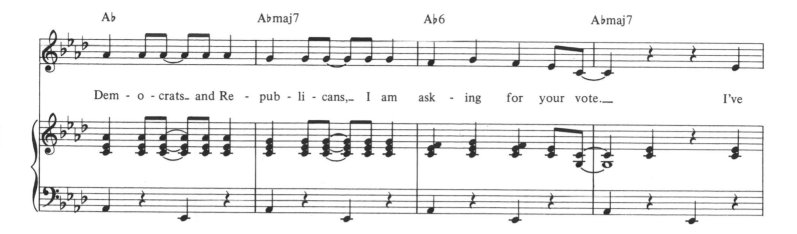

Dem - o - crats and Re - pub - li - cans, I am ask - ing for your vote. I've

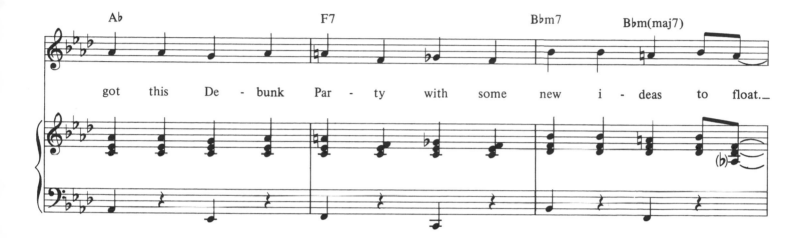

got this De - bunk Par - ty with some new i - deas to float.

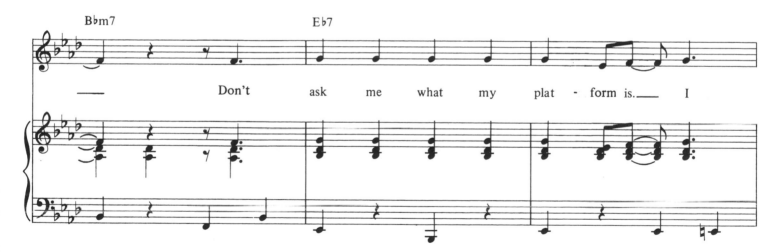

Don't ask me what my plat - form is. I

leave that stuff a - lone. 'Cause no one keeps those

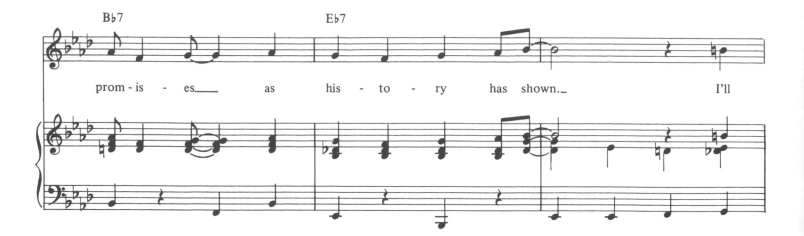

prom - is - es___ as his - to - ry has shown.___ I'll

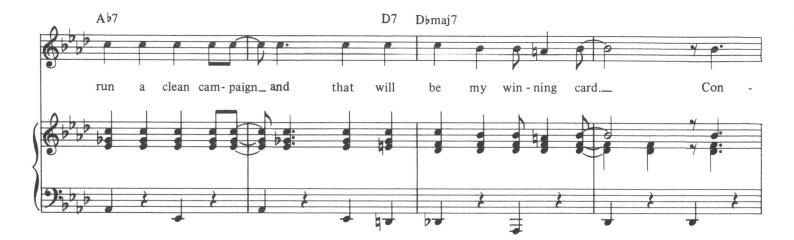

run a clean cam - paign___ and that will be my win - ning card.___ Con -

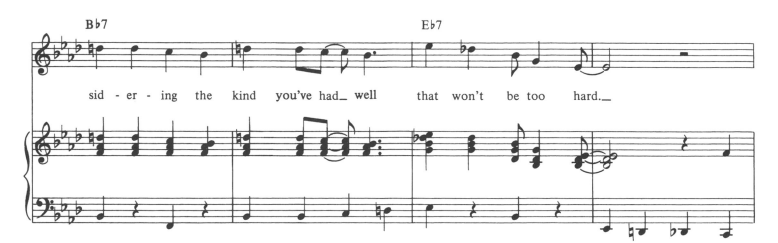

sid - er - ing the kind you've had___ well that won't be too hard.___

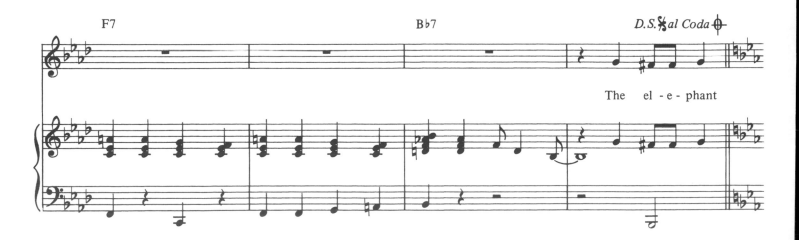

D.S. ℅ al Coda

The el - e - phant

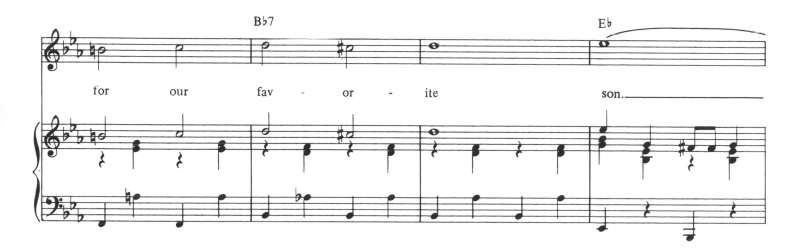

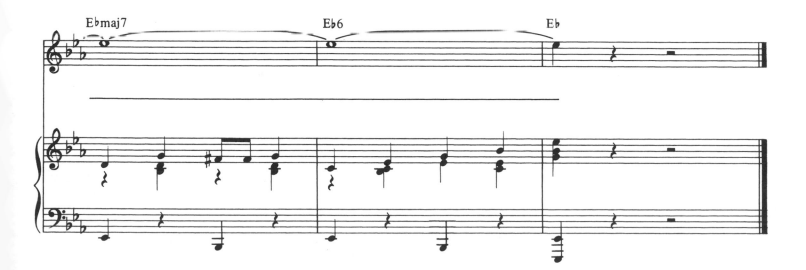

NO MAN LEFT FOR ME

Music by CY COLEMAN
Lyrics by BETTY COMDEN and ADOLPH GREEN

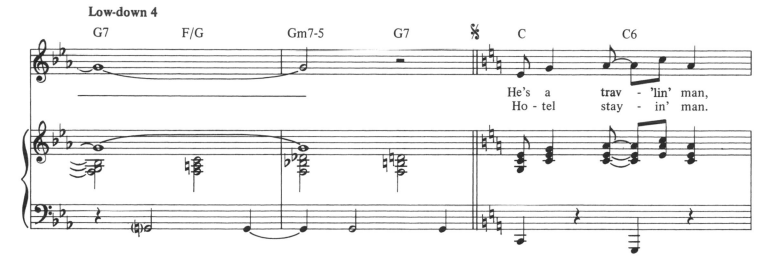

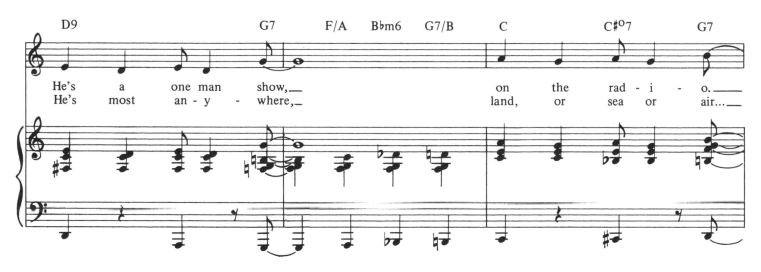

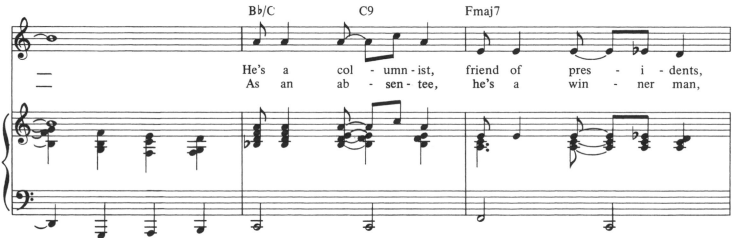

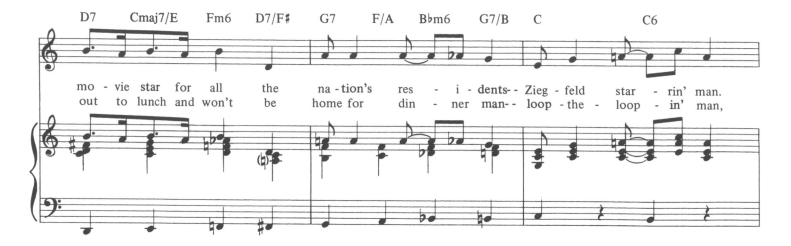

ev - 'ry time I start__ this feel-ing floods my heart,__ he needs me to feed the cat:__

__ Tho' when I'm by my-self I'm so lone-some,

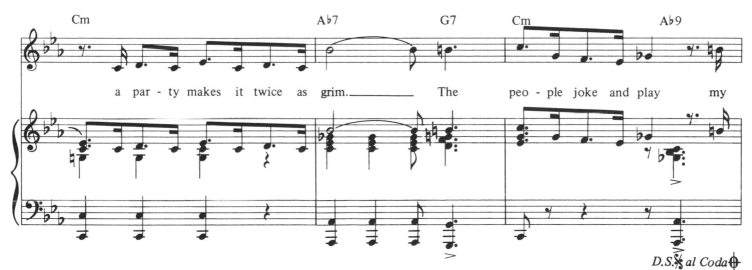

a par - ty makes it twice as grim._____ The peo - ple joke and play my

D.S. al Coda

mind is miles a-way,-- It's off on the road with him. __

NEVER MET A MAN I DIDN'T LIKE

Music by CY COLEMAN
Lyrics by BETTY COMDEN and ADOLPH GREEN

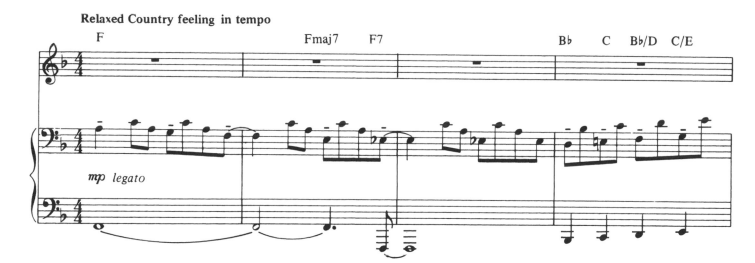

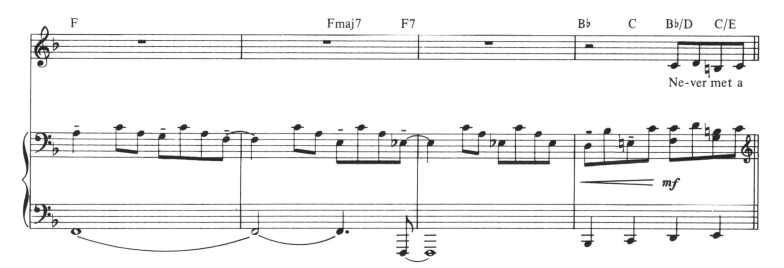

gent   or   Bow-'ry bum,__ Yes I've come__ a
Wales   or   work-ing Joe,__ Though I know__ life's

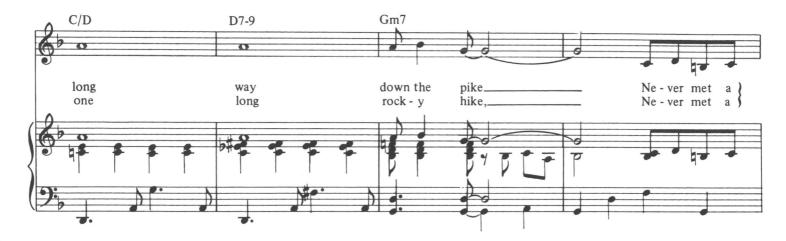

long   way   down the pike_____ Ne-ver met a
one   long   rock-y hike,_____ Ne-ver met a

man   I   did-n't like.__

Ne-ver shook a   did-n't like._____

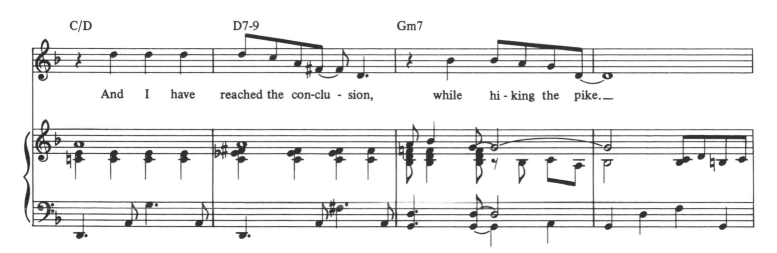

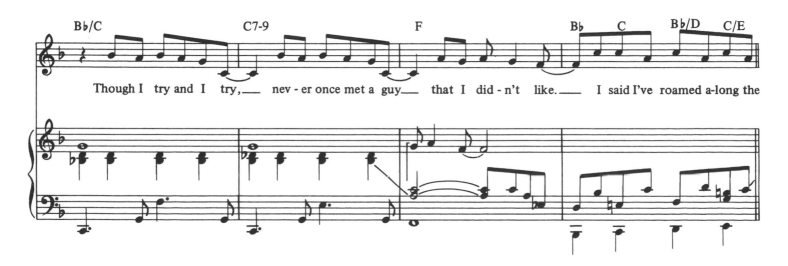

Na - pa Val - ley, Shu - bert Al - ley, Rue_____ de la Paix,__

O - kla - ho - ma and Ka - la - ma-zoo._____

And I have reached the con-clu - sion, while ma - king that hike,__

Yes, I'll say till I'm done,__ No, I nev - er met one__ that I did - n't like.__

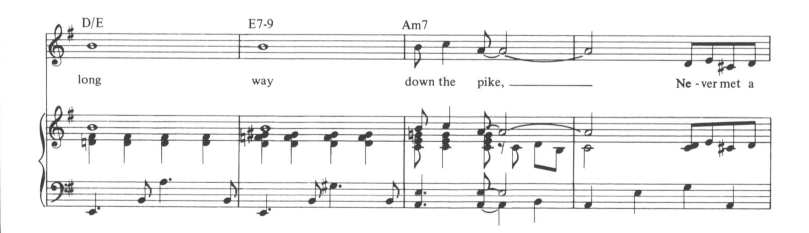

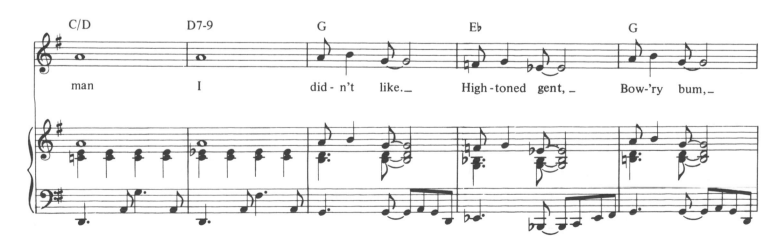

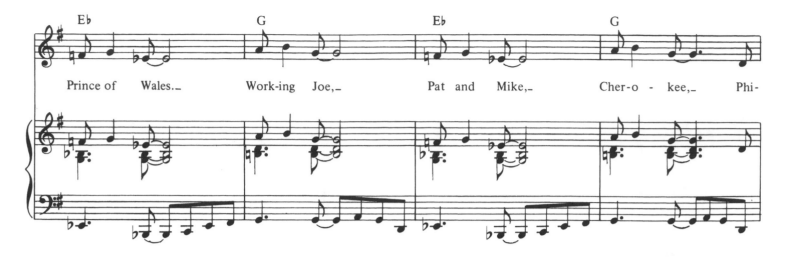

Prince of Wales.— Work-ing Joe,— Pat and Mike,— Cher-o - kee,— Phi-

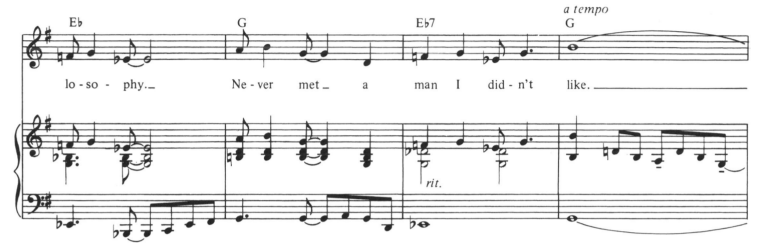

a tempo

lo - so - phy.— Ne - ver met— a man I did - n't like.—

rit.

Gmaj7   G7   C   D   C/E   D/F#   G

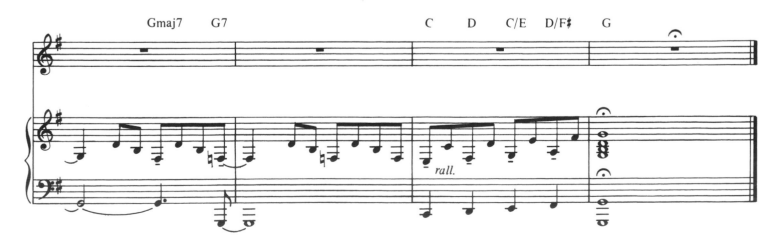

Gmaj7   G7   C   D   C/E   D/F#   G

rall.